T0087725

Bird on a Blade

ROSANNE CASH • DAN RIZZIE

BRAD AND MICHELE MOORE ROOTS MUSIC SERIES

University of Texas Press Austin

Printed in USA
First edition, 2018

Photographs by Gary Mamay and Rossa Cole

The paper used in this book meets the minimum requirements
of ANSI/NISO Z39.48-1992 (R1997) (Permanence of Paper).
♾

Design by Lindsay Starr

Library of Congress Cataloging-in-Publication Data

Names: Cash, Rosanne, author. | Rizzie, Dan, 1951- illustrator.
Title: Bird on a blade / Rosanne Cash, Dan Rizzie.
Description: Austin : University of Texas Press, 2018.
Identifiers: LCCN 2018017430
ISBN 978-1-4773-1821-8 (cloth : alk. paper)
Subjects: LCSH: Country music—Texts.
Classification: LCC ML54.6.C293 L95 2018
DDC 782.421642/0268—dc23
LC record available at https://lccn.loc.gov/201801743

FOR JOHN
AND
FOR SUSAN

This girl
This bird
who sings
She remembers
everything

We have been friends for many years, and almost since the beginning of our friendship, we have been musing about making a book together—one that would tie art and lyrics together in a way that encourages a fresh encounter with both. As the recording of Rosanne's album *She Remembers Everything* came to an end, the timing seemed perfect, and we got to work. For weeks, we dove into our own and each other's archives, pairing words and images, then refining and replacing and reimagining. Along the way, lyrics and pictures that we thought we knew well took on new meaning and resonance. It has been a privilege and a long-awaited dream to finally collaborate with each other on this book. The cross-pollination of visuals and language has inspired us deeply, and we hope it sparks a picture to your ear or a word to your image as well.

Rosanne Cash and Dan Rizzie
New York City, April 2018

Birdman

a Blade

a bird on the edge of a blade
lost now forever
my love
in a sweet memory

I sang my heart out for the crowd
asked forgiveness from them
then and now

pictures on the mantel
speak your name
softly like forgotten tunes
just outside the sound of pain

I just want a road that bends
a love that wins
an honest friend

all those who follow after
our children who we pledge
to historians and sailors
who float beyond the edge

We owe
everything
to this
rainbow of
suffering

this is my least favorite life
the one where you fly and I don't
a kiss holds a million deceits
and a lifetime goes up in smoke

Carol A

it's a hard road
but it fits your shoes

the ghosts have had their moment
now they fade into the sun
shining like the carousel
when summer's just begun

this is my least favorite you
who floats far above earth and stone
the night that I twist on the rack
is the time that I feel most at home

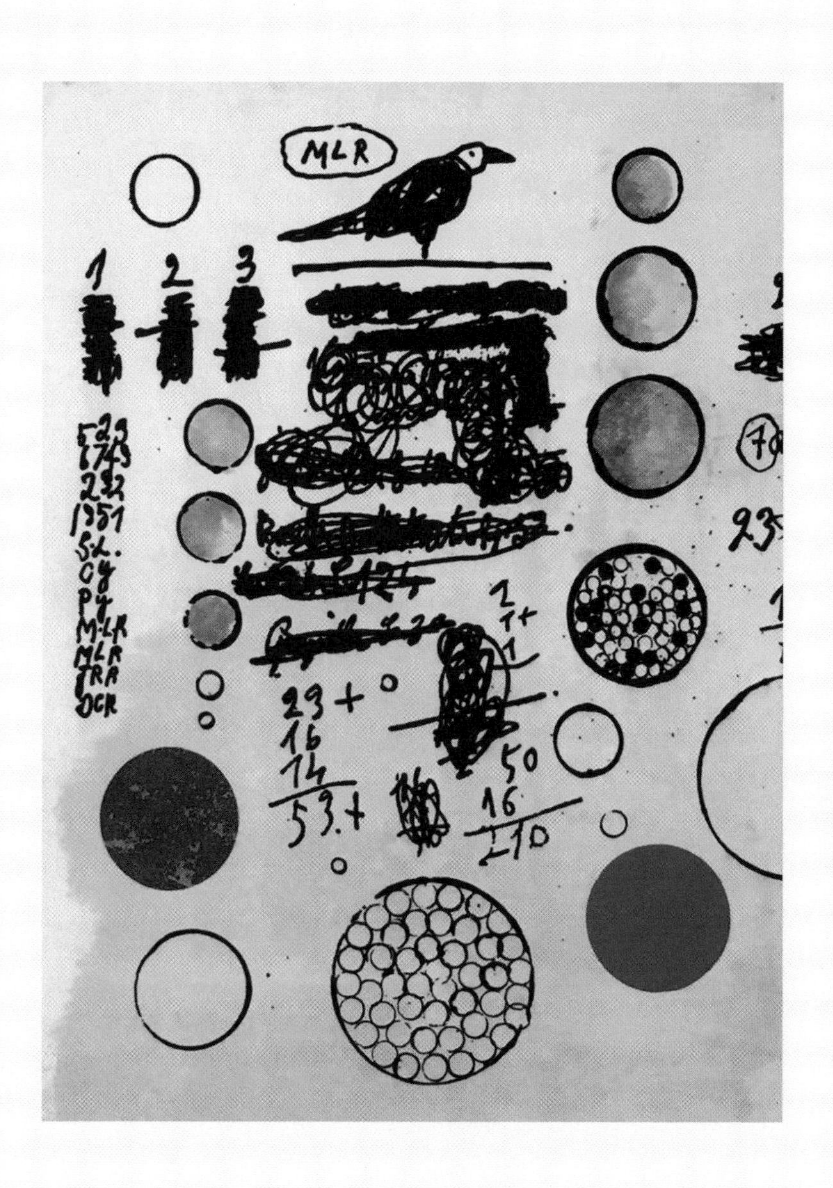
MLR
1
2
3
23 +
16
14
53.+
50
16

there was a time we looked so fine
behind a burning wall
of larceny and tenderness
we had to have it all

I'm the
sparrow on
the roof
I'm the list
of everyone
I have
to lose

no one sees behind the glass
no one knows I'm sinking fast
but soon we'll be sleeping in Paris
and we can set the angels free

you, in your light and glory
with your old dreams and epic stories
you seal all the darkened doors
and pull me up from the rabbit hole

time keeps slipping through the curtain
with the Empire State and small-batch bourbon

their little box of wishes
we want them to reach higher
just beyond their grasp
and plain desire

we're falling like the velvet petals
we're bleeding and we're torn
but God is in the roses
and the thorns

Somewhere
there's a quiet
room
where thieves
like us can
rest

we are awakened, restored and renewed
the bonds of desire have led me to you
the heat of the questions that linger and stir
is the fire that enfolds us, the place to be cured
salvation and rescue
and the one thing of which I am sure

I wish I was John Lennon
free as a bird
then all of you who sit and stare
would hang on my every word

the sun is on the cemetery
leaves are on the stones
there never was a place on earth
that felt so much like home

we're blinded by the beauty in our own lives
but I was taking all I could get
for five or six hours in the month of July
the summer I read Colette

there's a light inside a darkened room
a footstep on the stairs
a door that I forever close
to leave those memories there

His words are
cruel and
they sting
like fire
like the
devil's choir

there, behind the closing door
I'm not enough and then too much
our strange and beautiful lies
fade and turn to dust

DR14

we live our lives like fugitives
when we were born to live like queens

A
S
H

bells and roses
wake up the senses
to remind me who I am
bells and roses
the gifts of the spirit
shall not be squandered
on one man

DR99

it's a lonely world, just a numbers game
a hundred years will find me feeling just the same

dark highways and the country roads
don't scare you like they did
the woods and winds now welcome you
to the places you once hid

This is
our great
migration,
our mountain
and our
stone

the waves are breaking on the wall
the Queen of Roses spreads her arms to fly
she falls

how long was I asleep?
when did we plan to meet?
have you been waiting long for me?
when did the sky turn black?
do you still want me back?
I'll pick it all up piece by piece

DR10

don't send me no more letters
with your ignorance and rage
I don't want your tired religion
I'm not a soul you need to save

PIEGO RACCOMANDATO
PER POSTA
MINISTERO DELLE
FERROVIE DELLO

if Jesus came from Mississippi
if tears began to rhyme
I'll have to start at the beginning
it's a world of strange design

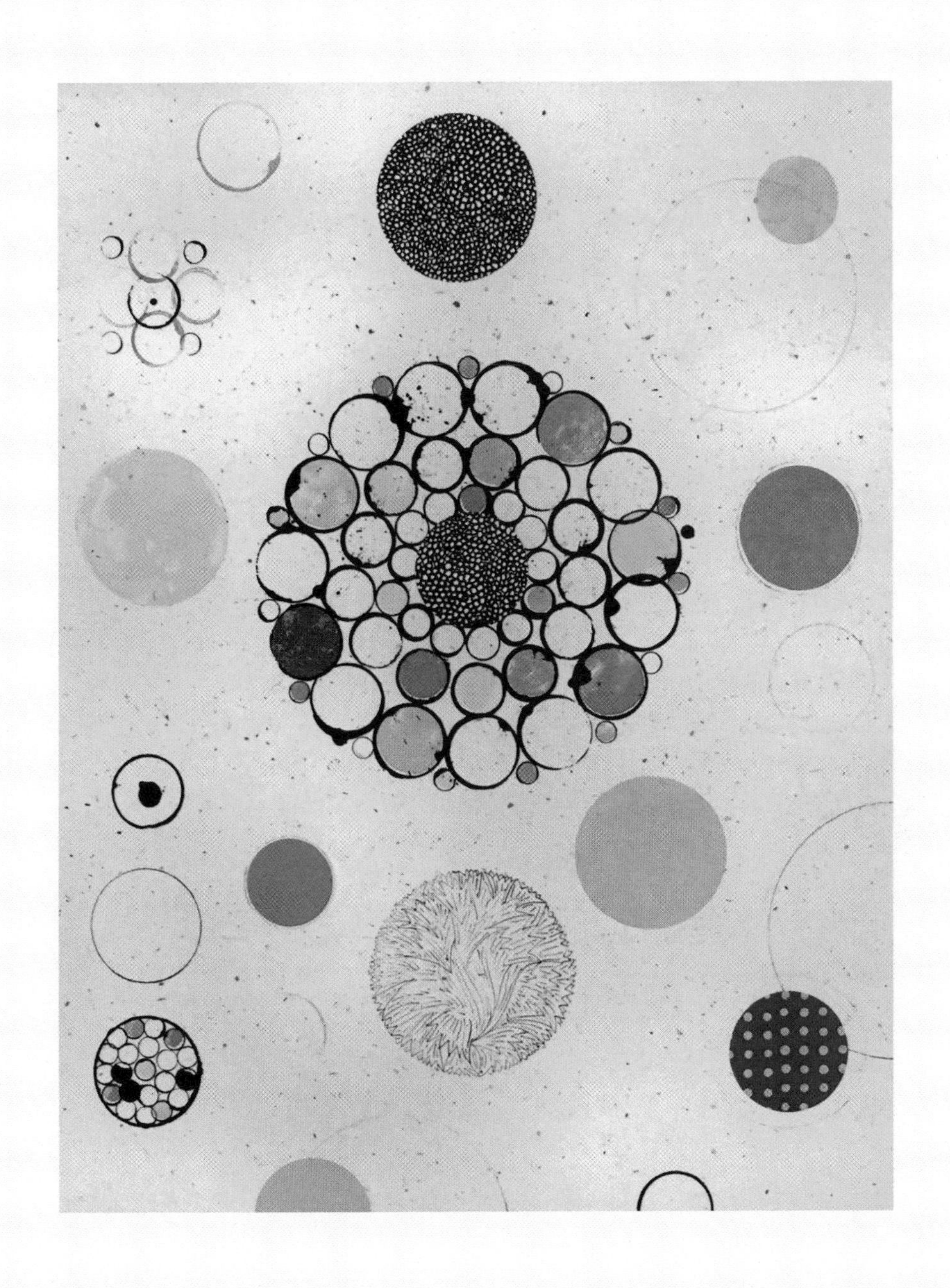

this room was filled with trouble
and sacraments deceived
now I'm a jewel in the shade
of his weeping willow tree

Look now
the curtain
rises,
it courses
through our
blood

when you're like a broken bird, tell heaven
battered wings against a darkened day

open up the window
hand the baby through
point her toward the ghostly bridge
and she'll know what to do

I will look for you
between the grooves of songs we sing
westward leading, still proceeding
to the world unseen

R

I walked around this world
bathed in neon and needing no one,
empty and disturbed.
yeah, I ran around this world
it nearly killed me but you can fill me
til I cry like a little girl

headlights on a Texas road
Hank Williams on the radio
a church wedding, they spent all they had
now the deal is done to become mom and dad

Citiz
AN
TEXAS
GAMES
COUNTY D

The mud
and tears
meet the
cotton bolls
it's a
heavy toll

I stand here by the western wall
maybe a little of that wall
stands inside of us all
I shove my prayers in the cracks
I got nothing to lose
no one to answer back

I keep my head down
I keep my eyes on you
it's a big wide world
with a million shades of modern blue

the world may just be spinning through us
and separation lets it show

well, you're not from around here
you're probably not our kind
it's hot from March to Christmas
and other things you'll find
won't fit your old ideas
they're a line in drifting sand
you'll walk across a ghostly bridge
to a crumbling promised land

we plow a similar field
of all the bones of remembered hearts
and all the crackpot dreams
and all the backroom art

it was a black Cadillac
that drove you away
everybody's talking
but they don't have much to say

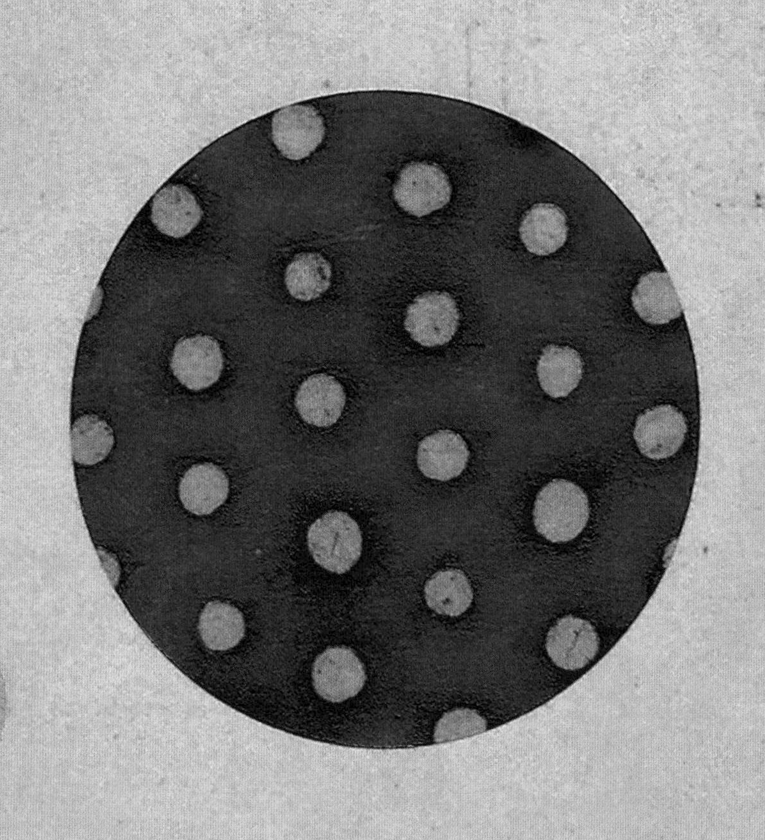

I. F. I.

M.P (8) - S. G. COUNIS.
La belle Grecque.
583 FIRENZE - Gall. Uffizi

Blue moon
out my
window
guess This
means
goodnight

Trombone
Carl Fischer, Inc. New York.

CREDITS

"Bells and Roses," "Black Cadillac," "Blue Moon with Heartache," "Dreams Are Not My Home," "God Is in the Roses," "I Was Watching You," "Last Stop before Home," "Like Fugitives," "List of Burdens," "Not Many Miles to Go," "Particle and Wave," "Rabbit Hole," "Sleeping in Paris," "The Summer I Read Colette," "Western Wall," "The Wheel," "The World Unseen," and "World Without Sound"

—

Written by Rosanne Cash
Published by Chelcait Music (SESAC)
All rights for Chelcait Music administered by Measurable Music LLC/Big Deal Music Group.

"Crossing to Jerusalem," "Everyone But Me," "Fire of the Newly Alive," "50,000 Watts," "The Long Way Home," "Modern Blue," "September When it Comes," "The Sunken Lands," "Tell Heaven," "The Undiscovered Country," and "World of Strange Design"

—

Written by Rosanne Cash and John Leventhal
Published by Chelcait Music (SESAC) and Lev-A-Tunes (ASCAP)
All rights for Chelcait Music administered by Measurable Music LLC/Big Deal Music Group.
All rights for Lev-A-Tunes administered by Downtown Music Publishing LLC.

"She Remembers Everything"

—

Written by Rosanne Cash and Sam Phillips
Published by Chelcait Music (SESAC) and Eden Bridge Music (ASCAP)
All rights for Chelcait Music administered by Measurable Music LLC/Big Deal Music Group.
All rights for Eden Bridge Music administered by Some Kind of Music LLC/Big Deal Music Group.

"My Least Favorite Life" and "The Only Thing Worth Fighting For"

—

Written by Rosanne Cash, T Bone Burnett, and Lera Lynn
Published by Chelcait Music (SESAC) and L-T Music Publishing (BMI)
All rights for Chelcait Music administered by Measurable Music LLC/Big Deal Music Group.
All rights for L-T Music Publishing administered by Universal Music Publishing.